D0116705

719 J4
14.50

H.R.H. Prince
Andrew
by Anwar Hussein

Hamlyn
London · New York · Sydney · Toronto

Contents

ACKNOWLEDGEMENTS
All colour and black and white photographs are by Anwar Hussein except for those on the following pages: Camera Press Limited 16 bottom, 20, 24, 40, 52, 55, 59, 60, 61 bottom, 67, 68/69, 71 top; Fox Photos Limited 15, 17; Popperfoto 4, 5, 9, 11, 12, 13, 14, 18, 19, 22; The Press Association Limited 16 top, 54 bottom, 58, 93 bottom; Syndication International Limited 21, 23, 35 bottom, 37, 44, 53, 54 top, 56, 57, 70, 92, 93 top.

First published in Great Britain 1979 by
The Hamlyn Publishing Group Limited
London · New York · Sydney · Toronto
Astronaut House, Feltham, Middlesex,
England

Created, designed and produced by Trewin
Copplestone Publishing Ltd, London

ISBN 0 600 37231 6

© Trewin Copplestone Publishing Ltd. 1979
All rights reserved. No part of this book may be reproduced or utilized in any form or by any means, electronic or mechanical, including photocopying, recording or by any information storage or retrieval system, without permission in writing from Trewin Copplestone Publishing Ltd, London, England

Phototypeset in Britain
by Keyfilm (Trendbourne) Ltd
Colour origination by Positive Plus
Printed in Italy by New Interlitho SpA

It's not hard to see why Andrew has attracted a film-star following among teenage girls. His casual good looks caused many female hearts to flutter at the 1978 Badminton Horse Trials.

DEDICATION

It has been a source of pride for me – as a photographer accredited to members of the Royal Family – to have been able in the course of my attendance at numerous royal events to chronicle, in some degree, the growing up of a young Prince. From all my professional experience, I can say that with his particular charm, Prince Andrew is one of the most natural people I could hope to have the opportunity of photographing. So now that the Queen's second son has, like all other British subjects when they reach their eighteenth birthday, legally come of age, I respectfully dedicate to His Royal Highness the following pages of informal photographs. They are a reminder of moments of relaxation and adventure, of interesting encounters and regal ceremonial and I hope they will give pleasure to readers all over the world.

Anwar Hussein

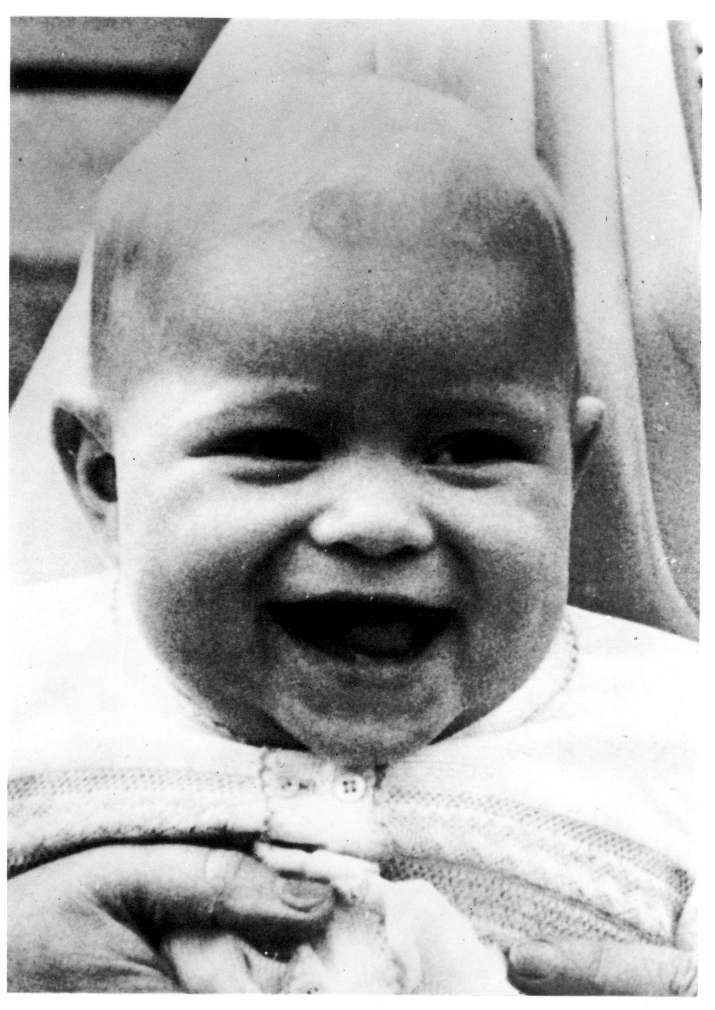

10

Early Years

I was so glad when I heard the news,
But still for all that I am so confused
Today, the nineteenth day of February,
The Queen gave birth to her third baby.
So we all should be proud and glad,
And sing her praises here in Trinidad.

This spontaneous tribute by a Trinidadian calypso singer indicates the delight with which the news of Prince Andrew's birth was received throughout the world.

Prince Andrew, third child of Queen Elizabeth II and Philip, Duke of Edinburgh, and second in succession to the British throne, was born on 19 February 1960. He was the first child to be born to a reigning British monarch in 103 years.

The Duke of Edinburgh was the first to be told of the birth, which took place in the Belgian Suite on the ground floor of Buckingham Palace, overlooking the gardens. Shortly after the birth, Prince Philip took Princess Anne to see her mother and new baby brother. He also telephoned Cheam School to inform Prince Charles, who arrived at the Palace that night to visit the Queen and the baby.

Opposite: At only six months old Prince Andrew is a happy, chuckling scene stealer delighted to pose for the photographer.

The Queen is caught by the camera as she prepares to lift Prince Andrew from his pram during a holiday at Balmoral Castle in Scotland.

12

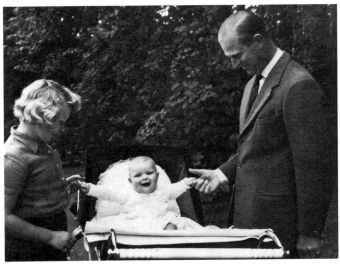

Opposite: Queen Elizabeth the Queen Mother holding a very cheerful Prince Andrew on her lap.

Top: A smiling baby Prince Andrew is held on his father's lap in this 'one for the family album' picture.

Above: Baby Prince Andrew seems delighted to pose for this photograph holding hands with his father and sister.

Right: A smiling two-and-a-half-year-old Prince Andrew plays with toys at Buckingham Palace.

Outside Buckingham Palace a crowd had been waiting with growing expectation throughout the sunny afternoon. Then, at about 4.15 p.m., a notice was posted on the railings of Buckingham Palace proclaiming:

'The Queen was safely delivered of a son at 3.30 p.m. today. Her Majesty and the infant Prince are both doing well.'

A cheer went up and within minutes buildings around the Palace were draped with Union Jacks and newsvendors were yelling 'Itzaboy'. There were big traffic jams in the West End of London as cars and thousands of pedestrians moved towards the Palace to celebrate the royal birth. They cheerfully watched the comings and goings of diplomats and other dignitaries bringing congratulatory messages to the Queen and Prince Philip on the birth of their second son.

The new royal baby weighed 7 lbs 3 ozs and had blue eyes and light brown hair. Journalists and broadcasters continued to refer to him as 'the infant prince' and the 'new royal baby' because for more than a month nobody but the immediate members of the royal family knew what the new prince was going to be called. It was not until the registration of the baby on 22 March that the public were to learn that the Prince had been given the names Andrew Albert Christian Edward.

The Queen and Prince Philip each chose two names from their families for the baby. He was called Andrew after Prince Philip's father, Prince Andrew of Greece. Albert was one of the names of the Queen's father, who was Prince Albert, Duke of York, before he became George VI. Christian was the name of Prince Philip's great-grandfather, King Christian IX of Denmark, and Edward was the name of the Queen's great-grandfather, King Edward VII.

There had not been a Prince Andrew in a British royal family for more than five hundred years. The last Prince Andrew had been a grandson of Robert II of Scotland, and since Andrew is also the name of its patron saint, Scotland should have felt pretty satisfied with the choice of name.

At his first Braemar Games in 1966 Prince Andrew is presented with a bouquet to give to his mother, which he carries rather self-consciously.

As a child Andrew was not often photographed at official functions, but this was an exception. Beautifully dressed in formal velvet and looking like a fairy tale prince, he already exhibits the composure expected of members of the royal family.

There was plenty of clowning around when Coco the Clown entertained at Prince Andrew's birthday party.

The camera has caught the usually smiling young prince in a contemplative mood.

The Queen wanted the children to have as normal a childhood as possible, and what could be more normal than being a Cub Scout?

Prince Andrew, like his elder brother and sister, was christened in the white and gold Music Room at Buckingham Palace. The room had been temporarily transformed into a chapel for the occasion. The baby prince was baptised on 8 April 1960 by the Archbishop of Canterbury. Over the years, royal christenings have become enveloped with family tradition. The same christening robe of Honiton lace, worn over a satin petticoat, has been worn by successive generations of the royal family ever since Queen Victoria's second child, Edward, was christened in 1842. And the same silver gilt font has been brought from the Gold Pantry at Windsor to wherever the ceremony is taking place.

Prince Andrew's christening was an intimate occasion, as were the christenings of the Queen's other children, with only relatives and close friends present. At the Queen's request, no pictures were taken at the ceremony for publication, which was a distinct departure from custom.

A Royal salute from Cub Scout Prince Andrew. For six months the First Marylebone Cub Scout pack was one of the most important in the country. It held its meetings at Buckingham Palace so that Prince Andrew could attend. Because Andrew enjoyed Cub life so much, a special Cub pack was formed at Heatherdown School when he began his first term there.

When Prince Charles and Princess Anne had been babies, the Queen's royal duties had led to the sacrifice of many of the pleasures of motherhood. Now the Queen made it clear that she was determined to allow her second son as much free-

dom as possible from the publicity that being a member of the British royal family involves. She kept the new baby strictly to herself. In fact, the Queen was so successful in shielding the infant prince from publicity that some people were asking if there was something wrong with Andrew, as so little had been seen of him.

There certainly wasn't anything wrong with the young prince. From very early on he showed signs of being the most extrovert and forthright of all the royal children. When Sister Helen Rowe, the midwife who helped to bring Prince Andrew into the world, gave a six-month progress report, she called him 'a baby full of smiles' and de-

scribed him as 'simply wonderful in every respect'. He was heavier than Prince Charles at the same age and, with a habit of curling his toes in pure pleasure and frequently splitting his face with a gummy smile, he had the sleek look of a baby who knows exactly where his next meal is coming from. He also took great delight in talking his head off without saying a single intelligible word.

The Prince's nanny, Mabel Anderson, found her charge of a remarkably placid dispostion, quite content to kick in his pram and hurl his silver rattle to be retrieved indefatigably by loving attendants, perhaps the most eager of whom was his sister, Princess Anne. She pleaded to be

Prince Andrew, binoculars at the ready, waits for Princess Anne to compete in the Windsor Horse Trials.

allowed to bath, feed and hold her baby brother, and spent many happy hours playing with him.

As Andrew grew older, he became an exuberant and mischievous youngster with a knack of getting his own way and a voice that even reticent household spokesmen were prepared to concede was of formidable volume. Once, when asked how old he was, he boomed, 'Three and a big bit.'

The Queen wanted him to be raised as normally as possible, so, as soon as he was old enough to toddle, she brought in other boys as playmates.

He started taking riding lessons in the Palace Mews, and at the age of four began lessons at Buckingham Palace with four children of friends of the Queen, and attended regular gymnastic classes.

All his young life, the lively Andrew found himself in and out of mischief. He seemed to delight in practical jokes, not always to the amusement of the recipients!

When he was big enough to drive a pedal car, he drove it at the royal corgi pack.

As soon as he could tie shoe laces, he tied together the boots of the guardsmen outside the Palace.

He poured bubble bath in the Windsor swimming pool.

He hid 'whoopee' cushions on the chairs to frighten his parents.

One night Prince Philip had to dash off to a public engagement sporting a black eye: Andrew had caught him a wallop during a bedtime bout of fisticuffs.

Oh, oh . . . this one got away! Young Prince Andrew chases a royal corgi puppy intent on catching up with the Queen.

Prince Andrew, like all small boys, is fascinated by water. He is especially lucky to have his own lake in the grounds of Buckingham Palace, where he can play with the royal corgis, Whisky and Sugar.

A royal tug of war at the railway station as Prince Andrew exerts his influence to get a royal corgi off the train. Eventually, the Prince was successful.

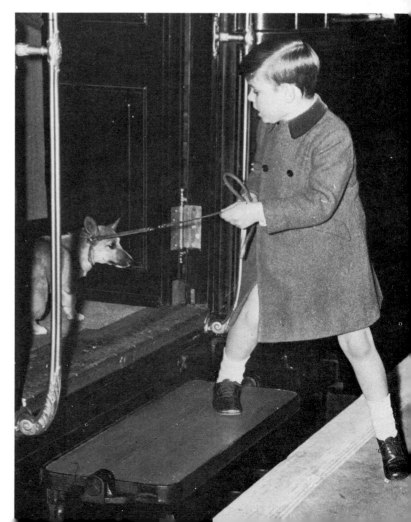

And on one occasion the spirited youngster was known to use one of the Queen's hats as a football!

When he was seven, Andrew became the proud owner of a £4000 version of James Bond's Aston Martin, which the Queen let him use only at weekends.

It had already become clear that Andrew Albert Christian Edward, second in line to the throne, was going to prove quite a handful.

Schoolbooks and Sniggers

The task of giving the young Prince Andrew his first lessons fell into the capable hands of Miss Catherine Peebles, otherwise known as Mispy. She was already quite an old hand at teaching the royal children, having started Prince Charles and Princess Anne on their academic careers. Beginning in May 1964 Andrew took daily lessons in the schoolroom at Buckingham Palace. By January 1967 he had risen to the rank of top monitor of the small, exclusive class. Among the privileges that this position entailed was the task of cleaning the blackboard – a highly coveted job. To prevent this 'duty' from going to his head, his jobs were also arranged to include tidying up when the other students had laid down their pencils.

When Andrew reached the age of eight, the Queen and Prince Philip decided that it was time for the young prince to exchange the comforts of Buckingham Palace for the more rigorous routines of boarding school life. Royal family and Palace servants alike had suffered enough from his overdose of high spirits, and everyone must have heaved a big sigh of relief when, in September 1968, he began his first term at Heatherdown, a private preparatory school near Ascot.

The announcement that Andrew should go to Heatherdown came as a surprise to the educational world, where it had been assumed that he would follow in Prince Charles's footsteps and go to Cheam.

One of the reasons that Heatherdown may have been chosen was because it was conveniently close to Windsor Castle. The school also had been attended by Angus Ogilvy, Princess Alexandra's husband, during his prep school days. He had been very happy there, a fact that might have influenced the royal family to some degree.

Before Andrew began his studies at Heatherdown, the headmaster, Mr James Edwards, expressed his hope that the young Prince would have a normal school life.

'It is a great honour for the school, but he will receive the same treatment here as all the other boys.'

On the subject of discipline, Mr Edwards said he expected the boys to be well-behaved. He was not opposed to corporal punishment, but administered it very seldom.

'Each child that I have is treated in a different way,' he said. *'Some might get beaten if the occasion arose, whereas with others it would do more harm than good. Some do prep in the evenings, others don't. They begin playing games like rugby when they are physically ready, not just when they reach a certain age.'*

A confident looking Prince Andrew strides across the grounds with his father on his first day at Heatherdown.

Nine-year-old Prince Andrew, followed closely by Prince Edward and Princess Anne, comes ashore from Britannia after a day on the fjords during the royal family's private visit to Norway.

As soon as lessons are over at Heatherdown, sporty Prince Andrew is often seen donning a pair of overalls over his uniform and joining his pals for a kickabout on the rugby field.

On 13 September Prince Andrew walked cheerfully into the world of dormitories, bells and conkers. The Queen and Prince Philip had brought their son overnight from Balmoral, where the family had been on holiday. The royal 'new boy', red cap in hand, grinned happily and gazed about him with obvious interest as he was taken into the school and introduced to his future classmates.

Andrew's life in the outside world had begun. His cheerful disposition helped him to fit in well with the new routine. Everyone got up at 7.15, had breakfast at 8 and lessons from 9 to 12.30. After lunch the boys played games in the afternoon – rugby, football, cricket or athletics. The boys went to chapel daily and were in bed by 8.10. Sundays were free, except for a short church service and a letter writing period. Each boy was expected to send one letter home a week.

When he was thirteen years old Andrew was ready to move on from prep school. The announcement that he was to go to Gordonstoun was rather lost in the high tide of reports about the plans for Princess Anne's wedding, but this did not diminish the importance of the decision to the young prince.

By going to Gordonstoun, Andrew was following in the footsteps of his father and his elder brother, Prince Charles. However, the school that was to mould the Prince was very different from the one that Prince Philip had attended forty years previously. Prince Philip in his day had to wear shorts in all weathers at this spartan school in Scotland. Herr Hahn, the school's founder and its headmaster for the first twenty years, was a man who believed education should be 'the modern equivalent of warfare – conquest without the humiliation of the vanquished'.

Prince Philip had been one of the first pupils at Gordonstoun, and a generation later Prince Charles found it still tough, a good training for the navy.

By September 1973, when Andrew first set foot within its doors, quite a few changes had taken place at the school. Short trousers, for example, were no longer compulsory and Andrew arrived wearing long grey trousers, slightly on the baggy side, as though his mother had insisted on allowing for growth – a problem faced by many a thirteen-year-old!

Also gone were the compulsory cold showers on freezing winter mornings. And it was no longer believed that an occasional drink or a cigarette would ruin a chap's stiff upper lip.

The biggest change of all was that now Gordonstoun, one of Britain's toughest boys' public schools, had graciously opened its classrooms to girls, and even accepted them as boarders!

As a result, many of the rules that Prince Philip and Prince Charles had been subject to had been relaxed, but Mr John Kempe, who took over as headmaster in 1960, claimed,

'It is the same school in spirit.' He went on to explain: *'We still have the training plan under which a boy has duties to perform and records that he has done them himself. He has to be seen to do them only if he is dishonest.*

'However, some of the details of the plan have changed. In Hahn's day people did press-ups and that sort of thing in the mornings.

'We just say that they are expected to have some exercise.'

It didn't take long for Andrew to settle into his new life at Gordonstoun and he seemed to get on well with the other pupils, even though a few of the boys were a bit cool towards him at first.

'I'm afraid he had a bit of "I am the Prince" about him when he first arrived,' said one friend, *'but he soon had it knocked out of him. You just cannot get away with that here. The ribbings he got were unmerciful. Andrew caught on fast. He had to.'*

But right from the start, the girls of Gordonstoun adored their royal classmate, and referred to him as 'super' and 'dishy'.

The boys too were soon won over by his easygoing manner and found themselves gravitating towards Andrew not because of his royal birth, but because he's enormous fun to be with.

The boisterous Andrew still managed to get into scrapes. Soon after he entered Gordonstoun, he landed in hospital for two days sleeping off the effects of a dormitory rag that had resulted in a crack on the head.

'It was just harmless horseplay,' said his housemaster. *'He joins in whatever goes on.'*

The young prince was, and still is, addressed by the staff as 'Prince Andrew', but when asked what the boys call him, one master laughed,

'Your guess is as good as mine. I can assure you they certainly never address him as "Prince Andrew" nor "Your Royal Highness". He's a very tough and independent young fellow. He has no time for sycophants. On the other hand, if anyone tries to take the mickey out of him, he doesn't hesitate to fight back. He's good – just as good – with verbalistics as he is with his fists.'

The Queen's no-publicity policy for both of her younger children has continued during Andrew's years at Gordonstoun. On a school visit to France he was known as plain 'Andrew Edwards' when he stayed with a local doctor and his family, which is an experience Prince Charles never had. Andrew was one of fifteen pupils from Gordonstoun who spent three weeks at a college in Toulouse to help familiarize themselves with the French language and to broaden their outlook on life. Thanks to the discretion of the French family with whom he stayed, his presence was not revealed and the Prince was able to follow the school's normal timetable and to go on a number of excursions, including visiting the local Concorde factory. During his stay he played football and scored a goal for Gordonstoun. Later, one French teacher was heard to remark: 'Mon Dieu! He certainly was a handful.'

Andrew obviously enjoyed travelling incognito and took delight in telling people, 'My father is a gentleman farmer, and my mother doesn't work.'

The college said that the Prince

'really enjoyed his stay, and showed keen interest in visiting the region, and learning its history. He certainly improved his French here in contact with our pupils, and the family he stayed with.'

Friends play an increasingly important part in Prince Andrew's life. He needs people to relax and have fun with, people who can forget his royal identity and accept him as an individual. Pupils at Gordonstoun say that he has plenty of boy and girl friends, but not just one close friend. One of the problems is that he is constantly being shadowed by a private detective, and though this doesn't seem to bother him, others find it takes some getting used to.

Andrew has a lot going for him personally, including undeniable good looks, an easy charm, a tremendous love of adventure and a fantastic sense of fun. He seems to have an inexhaustible supply of jokes.

'He never stops cracking them,' says one classmate. *'Goodness knows where he gets them from. But whatever the source, it shows no signs of drying up.'*

Friends play an important part in Andrew's life and at Lakefield he quickly became one of the lads.

Another schoolmate explained that Andrew became known as 'The Sniggerer' because of his tendency to sidle up to a chap and say, 'Have you heard the one about . . . '. The trouble is that by the time he's finished the joke he's laughing so much you can't understand a word of the punchline!

When Andrew was sixteen and in the fifth form at Gordonstoun, it was decided that he should spend two terms on an exchange visit at Lakefield College, seventy miles from Toronto in Canada. Andrew had been involved in the plan from the start and was very happy at the prospect. Lakefield is a spartan type school similar to Gordonstoun in many respects, and the Canadian and Scottish schools have had an exchange agreement for some years. In order to build a 'family

Proudly sporting his Lakefield College sweatshirt, Andrew waves to the crowd on the shore.

atmosphere', Lakefield likes to keep its number of students down to about 250. The outdoors is a large part of the curriculum. 'We try to foster a love of the outdoors and to teach the art of survival,' explained one official. The school is a huddle of wooden plank buildings. Students spend much of their time swimming, fishing, boating and canoeing. They constantly travel into the semi-wilderness area to the north, sleeping out in tents at least one night each week. The school also has long academic study hours, and the boys are expected to clean their own rooms and take turns waiting on table in the dining room.

Andrew's trip to Canada proved to be an enormous success. By the time he returned to England, his rough and tumble schoolboy image had vanished and he was a sophisticated scene-stealer. Right from the start the British prince had shown that he was perfectly capable of looking after himself. Before his arrival, the boys of Lakefield were waiting to knock a 'royal bighead' down to size, but instead they found themselves completely won over by his easy-going ways and endless enthusiasm for everything he did. On his introduction to the tough game of ice hockey, the Prince, much to the amazement of his fellow players, managed to score two goals. He also took more than his fair share of spills, which left him with a sore shoulder and a mass of bruises. 'He was pretty good. I was surprised,' admitted head boy David Miller. 'He was quite vicious too. You need to be a bit vicious to be good at this game.'

In Canada Andrew found that he had the freedom and opportunity to mix on equal terms with a group of young people from a totally different world who had no preconceptions or comprehension of the pressures and privileges of belonging to the royal family.

'The whole thing about Lakefield is the change,' explained Andrew. *'It is completely different from anything I have been used to.*

'The school is quite excellent and so are all the facilities that it offers. But it is not just that – the boys here are terrific, really great. They are different from the chaps in England because they have a different outlook from a different country.

'On top of all that everyone in Canada is incredibly friendly. You can say that life out here is very good indeed.'

When Andrew was at Lakefield College, he took time off from his studies to meet Canadian Prime Minister Pierre Trudeau and his family. The Prince obviously enjoyed their company, despite the cold.

A peaked cap shades his eyes against the summer glare as Prince Andrew, looking very much the seasoned explorer, arrives at the Coppermine River at the start of his canoe trip into the lonely Northwest Territory.

The highspot of Prince Andrew's stay at Lake-field was when he spent two and a half weeks on a trip to the Arctic region with four school friends and master Terry Guest. It was just the kind of adventure that the rugged Andrew loves, exploring the lonely Northwest Territory by canoe, sleeping under canvas at night, with the satisfaction of catching one's own food and not having to rely on the usual comforts of modern living.

Lugging your own kit is no problem when you're a sturdy six-footer. Here Andrew prepares for his adventure in the Arctic regions, the high-spot of his stay at Canada's Lakefield College.

With hands on hips and casually dressed, Andrew looks every inch the rugged adventurer as he waits to set out on an expedition to the Arctic.

He may be keen, but he's not careless. Here the young Prince makes an essential last minute map check before taking off for the lonely Northwest Territory.

Opposite: Andrew examines a canoe in a boathouse, and then prepares to take off on his adventure to the Arctic.

Andrew proves he's a good all-round sportsman as he takes to a canoe with Lakefield master Terry Guest.

After a trip to the exotic Arctic, Andrew heads down to the farm.

Prince Andrew relaxed in the quiet of the Canadian countryside during his Easter break from Lakefield College. He stayed on a farm eighty miles from Toronto owned by the family of a schoolmate.

He walked straight up to the first steer he saw and gave the animal a friendly pat on the head.

He tasted the maple syrup too!

The Prince took part in the wide selection of outdoor activities that the outward-bound style school encourages. He did particularly well in his sporting achievements.

'The Prince passed all his academic grades well enough, as you'd expect, but when he got into the arena or on those ski slopes, boy, he was really first class,' said Stephen Weir, one of Lakefield's civic leaders.

'I think you can say his stay over here in Canada was an unqualified success,' commented Stephen Weir. Everyone at Lakefield seemed genuinely sorry when it was time for their royal friend to return home.

Andrew returned to Gordonstoun with the intention of getting down to a bit of hard work. Though his tutors say he is a bright student, he can't afford to take it too easy. He has been described as 'non-academic' and his best achievements seem to have been in practical subjects such as woodwork and metalwork and, of course, in a variety of rigorous sporting activities. However, he has six 'O' levels to his credit (one more than his brother Prince Charles), in English Language, English Literature, Mathematics, French, General Science and British History. He is studying for his 'A' levels, which he will be taking in 1979. He realizes he must do well, for the results will certainly help in deciding his future. The subjects he has chosen are English, history and economics with political science. It had been thought that Andrew would be following his brother from Gordonstoun to Cambridge University, but Andrew wants to join the Royal Navy as a pilot when he leaves school, and his parents have agreed that he should go to the navy without going to university, subject, of course, to his passing the routine flying aptitude and medical tests. Those close to Andrew agree that he is better qualified as an athlete and adventurer than a scholar and he has never shown a great interest in pursuing an academic life.

Meanwhile Andrew is the glamour boy of the upper sixth at Gordonstoun. His appeal to girls is immense. His manners are impeccable and his sense of humour sparkles.

One thing we can be sure of, when Andrew does leave Gordonstoun, he will remember his school friends with affection. The jokes, the pranks and the interests they shared will not be forgotten in a hurry. And they, surely, will never forget him!

Prince Andrew chats with his hosts down on the farm.

Prince Andrew arrives home from school in Canada.

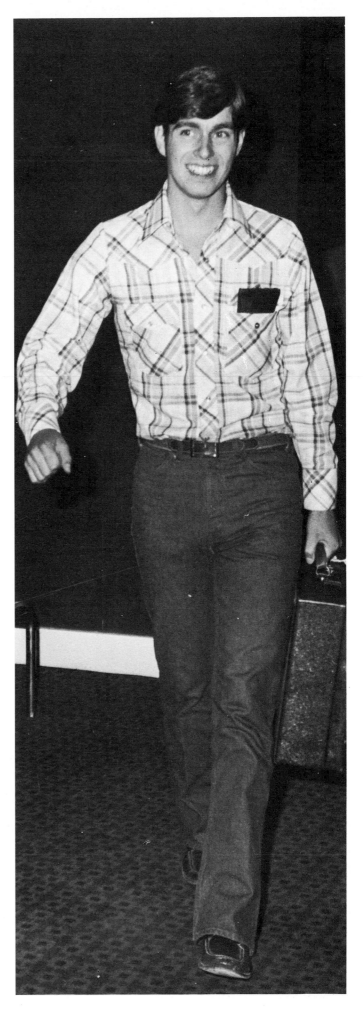

Prince Charming

It was at the 1976 Olympics in Montreal that Prince Andrew really emerged into the limelight for the first time. Suddenly, in Canada, the Queen found herself looking at her sixteen-year-old son with fresh eyes. Almost overnight, it seemed, the rather podgy rough and tumble schoolboy had undergone a considerable metamorphosis. Although Prince Charles, Princess Anne and the young Prince Edward were all at the Olympics too, it was the tall Andrew with his easy manner and captivating lopsided grin who set young female hearts aflutter.

Until then, it was Prince Charles who had always been cast as the charming and romantic royal star by the press. Now his younger brother was stealing all the attention. Girls of all ages were nudging each other and pointing at Andrew amidst giggles and whispered conversations. The interest was so intense that one British journalist was later heard to comment,

It was during the 1976 Montreal Olympics that Andrew first attracted the attention of the younger generation. Here he is touring the Olympic village with his mother.

It's that rugged outdoor-man look about Andrew that has the teenage girls screaming with delight.

'Andrew was the undoubted star – he was getting the attention normally reserved for pop-singers. He was pretending not to notice, but he was certainly well aware of what was going on!'

Thousands of teenagers with no great interest in sport as such came to the Olympic Games just to catch a glimpse of Prince Andrew. His adoring fans lined the routes in jeans and T-shirts, jostling more staid followers of royalty and elbowing hard-faced security men.

'He's marvellous – better looking than Robert Redford,' sighed one.

Astonished members of the royal party often found their progress impeded as letters were pressed into their hands addressed to the teenage girls' new idol. Inside were invitations to dates, complete with telephone numbers. Some had love poems and others contained photographs of the senders.

No matter where he appeared, all attention was focused away from the rest of the royal party and on to Andrew. His photographs, snipped from newspapers and magazines, became the pin-up on many a teenager's bedroom wall.

Without doubt, the most envied teenager during that Canadian visit was sixteen-year-old schoolgirl Sandi Jones. She became the Prince's official hostess when he visited the Olympic sailing site and was later at his side again at an official reception. Sandi, who was taken along to meet the royal family by her father, Colonel Campbell Jones, director-general of the Olympic yachting events, said simply, 'The Prince is very nice.'

One of her schoolgirl friends seemed far more impressed with Sandi's good fortune. 'She is the luckiest girl alive', she sighed. 'Just think, the last girl who acted as a hostess at the Olympic Games in Munich became the Queen of Sweden!'

Prince Andrew has a natural flair for being sociable. Even before he could walk, he waved to the crowds as he went by. He seems to mix easily with people from all sorts of different backgrounds, and has the habit of always stealing the limelight – sometimes without meaning to do so. All the ingredients that go to make up that indefinable quality of 'charisma' have blossomed in Andrew's personality. He always seems to know just how to behave wherever he is. With his jokes and frank open manner, he immediately puts people at ease and instinctively says just the right thing. One element of his charismatic appeal is that he is a tough, competitive sportsman; a man's man, who, in the company of women, has impeccable manners and a sparkling sense of fun.

And Andrew has made it quite clear that he adores the company of women. He is very aware of his appeal and he enjoys it. Although he does not have a steady girlfriend, his friendships with pretty girls have already earned the young Prince quite a reputation as·a charmer.

He has the girls at Gordonstoun in a real spin. One minute they believe they are establishing a relationship with him and the next he is moving on – fast.

'I know he's a bit of a flirt. But he really is the most charming person you could ever hope to meet,' declared one pupil.

'He's a great dancer,' said another. *'I've danced with him many times at the school disco and he's one of the best. But he dances with a lot of girls. He certainly knows how to spread himself around. Just*

Schoolgirl Sandi Jones was the envy of Canada when she became Prince Andrew's official 'hostess' at the Olympic sailing site.

as you think you are getting somewhere with him, he goes off with another girl. I suppose it is for the best really. If he ever stuck with one girl, she would be eaten alive.'

'He knows how to make you feel special though', added another. 'He's not a bit wet, which is a nice change round here'.

The Gordonstoun girls declare that Andrew is developing a rota of girls to take home to meet his family during the holidays. One young lady who seems to have had a fair share of visits to the royal households is eighteen-year-old Kirsty Richmond. Kirsty came into the romantic reckoning when she spent a night at Buckingham Palace after a weekend at Sandringham, the Queen's Norfolk home. Some months later she was seen in the Scottish Highlands, at Balmoral Castle, where the royal family were on holiday.

Blonde Kirsty comes from the Suffolk village of Great Barton, near Bury St Edmunds. Her widowed mother is a school nurse. Said a family friend, 'She has had to struggle to pay for Kirsty's private education. They are not particularly well off. Mrs Richmond has worked jolly hard as a nurse to make sure Kirsty could go to Gordonstoun.'

Kirsty Richmond, one of the teenage girls who has caught Prince Andrew's eye.

The girls of Gordonstoun claim that there is nothing serious between Andrew and Kirsty. For a time they seemed to think that Sue Barnard, a pupil from America, was the young Prince's favourite. Apparently, Andrew took Sue to meet the Queen during an autumn half-term holiday, but the press didn't get to hear of it at the time. When the news did get around, one Gordonstoun girl said,

'She is Andrew's long-term girlfriend. They've been going together for ages. Sue doesn't mind him taking Kirsty home because she knows that Kirsty is just a good friend. But the relationship with Sue has always seemed more serious to pupils at the school.'

Sue certainly wasn't the girl on Andrew's mind when he paid a visit to the famous London night-club 'Annabels', where he was refused admission until he put on a tie. With him then was Julia Guinness, a member of the famous brewing family.

And the appearance of another Gordonstoun pupil at a cross-country riding event in Warwickshire that Andrew was attending seemed to put an end to the idea that Sue Barnard was the eighteen-year-old Prince's regular date.

This girl in the Prince's life is Clio Nathaniels, an inseparable friend of Sue, who is now laughingly called 'one of Andrew's harem'. Friends have noticed quite a likeness between Clio and Sue. 'Clio is very popular,' said one of the girls, 'although she seems to be very shy.' Clio's parents left Britain to live in the Bahamas twenty years ago. Her father is an architect. From their home in Nassau, her mother said that she had been told that Clio had spent a weekend at Windsor with the royal family.

A romance? 'Oh, good gracious, no,' said Mrs Nathaniels. 'But she has written about him in letters home and we are delighted for her.'

On the question of a girl rota, a Palace spokesman would only say,

'He certainly does bring home friends every holiday. Naturally, just like any boy of his age, he wants his family to meet them.'

When Andrew returned to Canada to go to Lakefield College, he flew in to a pop star welcome. More than one hundred girls endured the freezing cold for hours to scream and blow kisses at their idol as he stepped from his plane at

Prince Andrew found many of the events at the Commonwealth Games of all-absorbing interest.

Toronto Airport. He then had to face the ordeal of giving his first press conference. One of the reporters present asked if he was interested in girls. 'What – is this the reputation I have?' replied the Prince in mock surprise. Then after some moments he added: 'I'm interested in Canadians – everybody.' When he was told that the Canadian newspapers were calling him 'Prince Charming' and comparing him to film idol Robert Redford, he rolled his eyes and said: 'Goodness . . . no comment . . . that's too dangerous.' He also refused to say what advice the Queen had given him before leaving England.

Andrew handled his first press conference masterfully. Without doubt, he enjoys being the centre of attention, and he enjoys having his photograph taken. One Canadian pressman said,

'The rewarding thing about covering Andy is that he doesn't mind standing around for a while while you fish around, searching for that one informal shot, bang, that's going to hit the front page.'

A relaxed Andrew enjoys chatting to an attractive young lady at Badminton Horse Trials.

Andrew was thrilled when he passed his driving test, and now drives himself around at every opportunity.

By the time that Andrew had settled in at Lakefield, a new phenomenon had emerged in Canada . . . a royal fan club.

'I'm an Andrew Windsor girl' was one of the most popular slogans that decorated the T-shirts of girls who had gathered in Lakefield for a glimpse of the handsome young prince.

When Andrew went down to Pittsburgh in the United States to cheer the Lakefield ice hockey team who were playing an away fixture, news got round fast that he was with the team. Within half an hour he was surrounded by girls – mainly the girlfriends of members of the Pittsburgh team.

'He really attracts the ladies,' said Al Pace, one of the Lakefield stars. *'I think some of the Pittsburgh guys were getting a bit worried. But the funniest thing was when one of the girls went up to her mother and told her there was a prince in the crowd.*

'The mother asked if it was an Arabian prince and the girl said, "Naw, mom, just the son of the Queen of England." '

Overleaf: Prince Andrew, living up to his image as Prince Charming, chats to the girls at a garden party in Victoria. He and Prince Philip had made a private visit to British Columbia while the Commonwealth Games were still in progress.

One seventeen-year-old schoolgirl, Helen Mac-murray, made a two hundred mile round trip to Lakefield from her Toronto home one weekend in the hope of seeing her idol. 'He's just so cute,' she explained. But her journey was fruitless: the Prince was away canoeing!

In spite of the privileges that accompany being second in line to the throne, Andrew does have his problems. Perhaps the most important one to a young man at his age is that his chances for a private date with a young lady are remote. He is shadowed constantly. His private detective must be only too aware of being the world's most un-wanted gooseberry!

Although Andrew accepts the fact that for his own safety a close watch has to be kept on him, and, indeed, he hardly seems to notice sometimes, there are times when even this easy-going young-ster feels he has to be alone. One such occasion occurred during Andrew's stay at Lakefield, when he again saw Sandi Jones, the girl he had first met at the 1976 Olympics.

First he invited pretty, blonde, pony-tailed Sandi to be his guest at a dance at his new Ontario school. Those who saw the young couple said, 'They looked as though they were made for each other.'

The tall and handsome Andrew laughed and chatted animatedly with Sandi and they danced together a number of times. At one point he put a protective arm round her shoulder.

Although there were many other girls present, Andrew stuck close to Sandi, who was wearing a silver-coloured jacket and red skirt. When they were not dancing, they munched doughnuts and sipped non-alcholic fruit punch. They left before the evening officially ended at 12.15 a.m. One of the girls present spoke for all her friends when she said, 'It was unfair he had a girl with him all the time. A lot of us would have loved to have asked him to dance.'

A spokesman for the school said, 'Sandi is about the only girl the Prince knew to invite – and she's damned pretty.' Two months later Andrew was seen in public with Sandi again. He took her to dinner at Toronto's Harbour Castle Hotel after going to a jazz concert. One of the usher-ettes at the concert said that the couple had sat at the back and slipped out before the end. 'We are not supposed to talk about them being here,' she added.

A spokesman for a public relations firm look-ing after the details of Andrew's 'educational' trip said, 'We assume he keeps in touch with Sandi. But I don't know how he liased with her.

The Prince at Windsor in a relaxed mood.

Obviously he had a date set up.'

After having dined and danced with Sandi, very much in public, the persuasive Andrew made a deal with his detective so that he could go skiing with Sandi – alone. The detective was naturally reluctant to let the Queen's son out of his sight, but finally gave in to his young charge when the Prince promised to keep a walkie-talkie with him. For once Prince Andrew was dating a girl without his every move being watched.

During Andrew's time at Lakefield, it wasn't only the Canadians who looked upon him as the royal heart-throb. America also woke up to the romantic appeal of the schoolboy Prince. One magazine, *Women's Wear Daily*, which is read by America's smart set, recalled that it seemed like only yesterday that Andrew was a toddler. Now, the magazine noted, 'he has stretched into nearly six feet of royal sex appeal.' Andrew, it said, has 'the most dazzling teeth this side of *Charlie's Angels.'*

It is clear that Andrew is going to become one of the most popular of all princes in the modern history of Britain. He has a flair for sharp dress-ing. He has a wardrobe filled with well-cut modern lounge suits and more casual clothes that ensure that he is a match for any trendy young man of his age. The fact that the Prince is very fit and has a fine figure also helps, of course. In fact, one modelling agency boss has said that Prince Andrew could get right to the top as a model. Mr Neville Gates, who runs the Nevs Model Agency added, 'He's got real style. We could make a fortune with him.'

After years of appearing in newspaper stories as the 'Clown Prince' because of his active and delightful sense of humour, Andrew has gradu-ated to the role of royal pin-up. It's not hard to see why this blue-eyed six-footer with his mop of elegantly untidy hair has earned film-star appeal. Even at Prince Charles's much publicized thirtieth birthday party at Buckingham Palace, it was younger brother Andrew who seemed to steal the show. He and Prince Edward were given special leave from Gordonstoun to attend the party. Although Andrew had injured his foot on the rugby field and had to hobble into the Palace ballroom clutching a walking stick, he was soon limping round the dance floor with every lovely lady in sight, including Prince Charles's girl-friends.

He whirled his walking stick around like Charlie Chaplin and announced, 'I've fractured my foot.' A Palace spokesman said that the injury was not serious, but 'for the party he had to wear more comfortable slip-on shoes than the formal ones normally worn with a dinner jacket.'

'For He's a Jolly Good Sport'

Prince Andrew enjoys sporting activities whole-heartedly. His confidence and natural skill in the world of sport developed early. He had his first riding lessons when he was only two years old, Prince Philip taught him to swim in the Palace pool when he was just three, and by the age of four he was going to weekly gymnastics classes.

He soon proved to be a fearless sportsman. Roy Lee, who taught the young prince to ice skate, remembers:

'He was only about seven or eight, but already he had a very striking personality. Full of fun. I think he must have been a bit of a mischievous little fellow because on the first visit to the ice rink his nanny said I mustn't let the Prince have all his own way.

'What worried me was that, like most young children, he was absolutely fearless on the ice. Children have no thought about falling. All they want to do is speed across the ice, fast as they can go. I remember feeling a bit sick inside as I watched him, thinking, "I hope he doesn't crack his head or something, otherwise I'll be sent to the Tower." He did have one or two spills. No matter. He got up and carried on. In all he had about eight half-hour lessons. Each time the rink would be cleared of members of the public and Prince Andrew would have the place to himself. Apart from myself the only other people present were his bodyguards. Some guarded the rink, others kept watch from a balcony.

'Towards the end of the course, the Prince called to one of the bodyguards, "Hey, look at me, I can skate by myself." I don't know who was more proud, the Prince or me.'

Today Andrew is a cracking all-round sports-man, which isn't surprising considering that he received tennis coaching from Dan Maskell, former Wimbledon champion and top BBC commentator. He received cricket tips from Len Muncer, the head coach at Lords, and the late Graham Hill taught him to drive on the royal estates' private roads. No wonder he passed his driving test at his first attempt!

His father taught Andrew to sail at Cowes. And Cowes week provides a perfect atmosphere for Andrew. Some 4000 yachtsmen converge on the Isle of Wight each year. The sailing is expert and the competition keen. The young prince also thoroughly enjoys sailing with his family. He has a light aluminium craft, which travels on a trailer when the family are at Balmoral.

Looking very serious for his thirteen years, Prince Andrew goes yachting at Cowes with his father.

Opposite: Wherever there are sports you'll find Prince Andrew. This time a spectator, he bites his lip in suspense as he watches Princess Anne and Captain Mark Phillips compete at the Badminton Horse Trials.

During the holidays Prince Andrew has learnt to fish and shoot and he has put in several winters on the ski slopes, which proved a useful accomplishment when he went to Lakefield, in Canada. At Lakefield he also proved to be pretty fearless on the bobsleigh.

The list of sports in which the distinctly robust Andrew likes to participate is almost endless. He's good at squash. He plays a tough game of soccer and is an enthusiastic supporter of Bolton Wanderers. One of his prize possessions is a supporter's scarf sent to him as a Christmas present. He has proved himself a useful full-back at rugby, and his opponents fear his hard tackling.

The prince shows that Britons still can rule the waves, as he goes canoeing in Canada.

'Down to the sea . . .'. Appropriately dressed for boating, Andrew lends a helping hand with the dinghy.

Just as much at home on water as on land, Prince Andrew prepares to take part in the National Flying Fifteen Class Tudor Rose Challenge Bowl of the Cowes Regatta.

There he goes . . . royal rugger star Prince Andrew delights his fans in Ontario.

Prince Andrew enjoys a joke with his instructor, Flight Lieutenant Bullivant, before their glider is launched.

He made his first glider flight, a four-minute circuit of the Milltown Airfield in Morayshire, in a two-seat trainer when he was just fifteen. Flight Lieutenant Sandy Reid, in charge of the gliding school, commented: 'Andrew is very quick to learn and is fearless.'

One Royal Air Force spokesman had described the experience of gliding:

'When you're up there in the clouds, and the hot-air currents come punching up at you from the ground and send you soaring away like mad, then there's only one boss and that's God.'

This rewarding and sobering experience is obviously one of the reasons for Prince Andrew's new found maturity.

When he was sixteen he flew solo for the first time, as part of his Air Training Corps activities at Gordonstoun, and gained his ATC gliding proficiency wings. His instructor, Flight Lieutenant Peter Bullivant described the Prince as an enthusiastic and very good pilot.

Andrew was thrilled at having gained his wings and was quick to point out his achievement to Prince Charles, who is himself a competent jet and helicopter pilot. A senior RAF spokesman testified to his delight: 'He couldn't wait to chide his brother. "Now I can do something you can't do," sort of thing.'

In the spring of 1978 Prince Charles suggested that Andrew should enrol in a special course to gain his parachute wings at Number One Parachute Training Centre, RAF Brize Norton, during the Easter holidays.

Prince Charles is Colonel-in-Chief of the Parachute Regiment. He had made a jump into the sea seven years previously, but he now felt he should take a more intensive course. So, at the same time that Prince Charles undertook his training course, his younger brother participated in a beginners' course at the same airfield.

Bad weather kept the brothers on the ground longer than they had anticipated, but they made good use of the extra time, including practice falls, mock exercises and jumping from a captive balloon.

Finally, Andrew was ready to make a series of 1000 foot descents from Hercules aircraft, and he was determined to get in a jump ahead of his elder brother. The news media were there in force and twice had the opportunity of witnessing the jumps. During the first of these public jumps, the young prince got his feet twisted in the lines of his parachute. He had to spend time kicking himself free and clearing his lines, but, true to form, he remained calm throughout and everyone breathed a sigh of relief as he landed safely on firm ground.

A look of delighted triumph lights Prince Andrew's face after he completes his first solo glider flight.

Just hanging around . . . Prince Andrew in a mock parachute during training.

In April 1978 Prince Andrew was awarded his parachute wings after completing a course at RAF Brize Norton during the Easter holidays. Prince Charles, who is Colonel-in-Chief of the Parachute Regiment, was undertaking a course at the same time and there was much friendly rivalry between the brothers.

Above: The camera seems to follow him everywhere, but has to settle for this on-the-ground shot as Prince Andrew strides off for another parachute jump.

Smiles all round as Prince Andrew shows his Certificate of Competence to RAF officers.

A Prince and His Family

Prince Andrew is twelve years younger than Prince Charles, and four years older than Prince Edward, the Queen's youngest child. Despite this age difference and the fact that the Queen's four children are very different in temperament (or perhaps because of it), they all get on well together and are a very close family.

From a very early age Andrew showed signs of being the most individualistic of the Queen's children, including the highly independent and outspoken Princess Anne. He was an irrepressible, mischievous youngster, always getting into scrapes. Whereas his father has described him as a natural boss, his mother once commented, 'He is not always a little ray of sunshine.'

Prince Charles and Princess Anne were thrilled at the birth of their younger brothers, playing with them and keeping a watchful and affectionate eye on them. With an immensely popular brother like Prince Charles, it can't have been easy for the young Andrew to make his own mark on the world. But he needn't have worried. Already he appears to have at least as much self-assurance as his elder brother had at the same age. For example, no one had to persuade the outgoing Andrew to attend the tough Lakefield College in Canada. He was raring to go and prove to everyone that he was quite capable of looking after himself.

Andrew and his younger brother, Prince Edward, are as different as chalk and cheese, but they get on well together. Edward is four years younger than Andrew and appears to be as quiet and shy as Andrew is lively and gregarious. He is said to be much more studious than any of his brothers or his sister. Like Andrew, Edward went to Heatherdown Preparatory School near Ascot, and then followed him to Gordonstoun.

The royal family always feels very much at home in Scotland, and they all can often be seen wearing the traditional kilt, as here at Braemar.

Christmas is a time when all the family get together. Here they attend a Christmas Day church service at Windsor.

Overleaf: Prince Andrew comes ashore from the Royal Yacht Britannia to greet his two brothers, Prince Charles and Prince Edward, who had flown out to join the rest of the royal family at the 1976 Olympic Games.

Above, they are all seen together at Bromont in Canada.

Another member of the family of whom Andrew seems particularly fond is his cousin David, Viscount Linley, the son of Princess Margaret. The two boys were confirmed together on 13 April 1976 in St George's Chapel at Windsor Castle in the presence of many members of the royal family. David and his sister, Lady Sarah Armstrong-Jones, have spent several holidays with Andrew and his family, and are often seen together in public at events such as the Badminton Horse Trials.

The Duke and Duchess of Kent's eldest son, George, Earl of St Andrews, is another contemporary whose company Andrew enjoys. He won a scholarship to Eton when he was twelve and is considered the intellectual of the royal family. He and Andrew have been noticed immersed in long conversations, which perhaps give this lively prince an opportunity to indulge the more serious, contemplative side of his nature.

Prince Andrew seems to have inherited a fascinating mixture of characteristics. Like his father, he is extremely physically active. It has often been noticed that father and son have the same ramrod stance and raking walk, with their hands often clasped behind their backs – a posture we have come to identify with all the men in the royal family. They also seem to share a tough, adventurous approach to life.

From his mother, the boisterous and extrovert young prince appears to have inherited the fine quality of sensitive insight. Combined with a maturity unexpected in one so young, and the social graces that seem instinctive to him, Andrew appears to be almost a natural diplomat.

Two attributes that contribute to Andrew's extremely attractive personality are his warmth and natural crowd-pleasing charm. In this manner he obviously takes after his grandmother, the Queen Mother, of whom he is extremely fond.

Although Andrew is a young man anyone would be glad to have as a friend, it must sometimes be difficult for him to relax completely in other people's company. He realizes that he must be careful what he says about himself, his family, or any subject of public concern. For this reason Andrew particularly enjoys the company of his family, and especially of those who are members of his own generation. Among them he can relax and feel comfortable, knowing that they all understand and share the problems that being a royal involves.

Opposite: Andrew and Anne, watching the progress of the game as critically as anyone in the kingdom.

66

Whenever possible Prince Andrew joins other members of the royal family at major royal ceremonies, such as Trooping the Colour, which takes place each year on the sovereign's official birthday, a Saturday early in June. It is a traditional ceremony with origins that stretch back over many years and is looked upon as one of the most impressive and colourful ceremonies in the royal calendar. The sight of the Queen, riding side-saddle accompanied by her Household Cavalry, the stamp of the soldiers' boots, the yells of command from sergeant major, and the music of the massed bands has always excited onlookers – including the Queen's children. After the ceremony the family congregate on the balcony of Buckingham Palace and watch the fly-past of the Royal Air Force.

Perhaps the most impressive royal ceremonies

took place in the Queen's silver jubilee year. Prince Andrew flew back from Canada to take part in the Queen's Silver Jubilee celebrations. On Monday, 6 June, the eve of Jubilee Day, he accompanied the Queen when she drove along the Long Walk to Windsor Great Park to light the first in a chain of bonfires. Within an hour the bonfire in Saxavord in the Shetlands, the northern-most point of the network of 102 beacons, was

Andrew has inherited his grandmother's immense charm. Here the Queen Mother and her grandson make their way to church at Badminton.

ablaze. For most people, it was this bonfire cere-mony that really brought the Jubilee alive.

That night too thousands of eager sightseers and royalty watchers camped on the streets of London in order to lay claim to good vantage points for the Jubilee Day procession. The fact that there had been showers in London through-out that Monday did not dampen their spirits in the least and when the royal family arrived at Buckingham Palace from Windsor at about mid-night, there were shouts of 'We want the Queen'.

The first coach, containing Princess Anne and her husband, Captain Mark Phillips, left Buck-ingham Palace just after 10.25 a.m. on Jubilee Day to the cheers of the crowd. Prince Andrew and Prince Edward were in the seventh coach accompanying the Queen Mother. Finally, Her Majesty the Queen with Prince Philip beside her came through the centre arch of the Palace in the magnificent Golden Coach. More than five hundred million people watched the pomp and pageantry, their eyes glued to their television sets.

During the Jubilee Day service at St Paul's Cathedral the royal family sat on both sides of the aisle in the front row. The Queen Mother, in autumn yellow, could often be caught glancing proudly at her grandsons beside her.

Queen Elizabeth, the Queen Mother, poses arm-in-arm with her grandsons Charles and Andrew.

Prince Andrew, with Prince Edward at his side, follows the Queen Mother and Prince Charles down the steps of St Paul's after the Queen's Silver Jubilee Day service. Below: riding in the procession to St Paul's.

On the Queen Mother's seventy-fifth birthday Prince Andrew gave her two pottery dishes that he made at school. They obviously met with her admiration when he visited her in the grounds of her country residence.

When the royal family returned to the Palace, an enormous crowd of more than 100,000 people had gathered in front of the railings and roared for them to come onto the balcony, which, of course, they did.

Of course, all the members of the royal family look forward to the times when they can be together out of the gaze of the public eye. For about three months of the year they are able to 'get away from it all' at Balmoral Castle in Scotland, and Sandringham House in Norfolk.

There is little doubt that Balmoral Castle is the family's favourite home. With its acres and acres of heather and woodland, its rivers and nearby lochs, it is the perfect place to relax. It was here that Prince Andrew learned to drive, and here that he can sail with friends, play golf on the private course, or see a film in the castle's own cinema. The family are usually at Balmoral from August until October.

In recent years Christmas has been spent at Windsor Castle. Before that the family had always gone to Sandringham, but, after the birth of Prince Andrew and Prince Edward, and their cousins, it was decided that there would not be sufficient room for the whole family to gather at Sandringham for the traditional Christmas. And, because the royal family feel it is very important to be together at Christmas, Windsor was chosen as an alternative venue. Because it is so near to London, Windsor Castle has become a regular weekend home for the Queen and her family and friends are often invited to stay. Although the castle contains priceless art treasures of every description, guests are struck by the unpretentious way of life there. They can relax in the swimming pool or make use of the badminton court. The private apartments are bright and cheery with every modern convenience, including stereo equipment cleverly concealed inside antique furniture.

The Queen and Prince Philip find it hard to keep a straight face when in the company of their second son. Here, at the Badminton Horse Trials, Andrew lives up to his reputation as 'the joker in the royal pack'.

During the Olympic Games Prince Andrew travelled with his mother to Bromont to watch the equestrian events. They were met there by Prince Philip. Prince Charles and Prince Edward also flew out from England to watch Princess Anne, who was representing Britain in the Three-Day Event. Unfortunately, the cross-country proved difficult going. The morning had started with a storm and the Princess's horse slipped in the boggy ground approaching the nineteenth fence, dropping her to the ground.

Andrew, accompanying his father on a visit to British Columbia, waves to the crowd.

Andrew roars with laughter as Margaret Trudeau mops up a spill at an official occasion during the 1976 royal visit to Canada.

Andrew towers above his mother at a state banquet given during their visit to the Commonwealth Games in Edmonton.

Andrew finds great comradeship in his close family. Here in Canada he shares a quiet moment with his mother and brother.

Prince Charles and Prince Andrew arrive at the world famous Calgary Stampede in an open horse-drawn carriage. Prince Charles officially opened the show, but Andrew stole the limelight from his older brother!

Here Prince Andrew exhibits the impeccable manners of a royal gentleman: at the film premiere of 'International Velvet', he gets out of the car first, and then steps aside to let the Queen pass.

Without doubt the Queen and her family are country folk at heart and they love the life that their country homes offer them. The New Year holiday is spent at Sandringham, which stands in 20,000 acres on the flat, windswept coastal edge of Norfolk about 110 miles north-east of London. Here the family can go shooting, riding, trudging across ploughed fields in wellington boots or whatever else may take their fancy. As at Windsor Castle and Balmoral, friends are often invited to join in the family's activities. Evening is a time when everybody gets together for friendly family chats around log fires or to watch television or a specially screened film.

The public can surely appreciate that the Queen and her family, so often in the public gaze and separated in the line of duty, thoroughly deserve this period of private togetherness.

The Understudy Prince

As royalty-watchers point out, Prince Andrew is only heartbeats away from the throne!

It cannot be forgotten that the last two crowned kings of England, George V and George VI, were both second sons. George V had to take over at the death of his older brother the Duke of Clarence. And the Queen is anxious that there should be no repeat of the dilemma that faced her father, King George VI, who was totally unprepared for the throne when his brother, Edward VIII, abdicated. She has made certain that Andrew has been made fully aware of his role as understudy and that if it were necessary, he would be ready and trained to step into Prince Charles's shoes.

Prince Andrew would accede to the throne only in the unlikely event that Prince Charles is prevented from doing so for any reason, or abdicates or leaves no heir. Assuming, however, that Prince Charles does become king, his younger brother, whose education and training have been designed to prepare him for royal duties, will prove an ideal right-hand man.

When Prince Andrew reached the age of eighteen, he became entitled to a £20,000 a year income from the Civil List (which is a public salary), but the Queen decided that her younger son will get only pocket money. A Buckingham Palace spokesman said,

'Because Prince Andrew is still at school and is not undertaking royal duties, he will only receive an amount appropriate to a schoolboy. The bulk of the money will be held on his behalf by the Royal Trustees, the Prime Minister, the Chancellor of the Exchequer and the Keeper of the Privy Purse.'

Although Price Andrew plans to join the Royal Navy when he leaves school, the question of increasing his allowance has not yet been discussed.

The news that Andrew is hoping to become a pilot with the Royal Navy must have pleased Prince Philip, who has always encouraged his sons to follow his example by joining the Senior

While on holiday at Balmoral the royal family always makes a point of attending the Braemar Highland Games. These two little girls will never forget the day they came face to face with not one but two Prince Charmings.

Service. It is a long family tradition and Andrew obviously has also been influenced by his elder brother's success in the forces. His grandfather, King George VI, fought in the First World War in the Battle of Jutland and his great-uncle Earl Mountbatten of Burma also had a distinguished naval career.

It is generally agreed that the Royal Navy will be able to provide Andrew with an outlet for his adventurous, extrovert nature. His father describes him as 'a natural boss', which should make him good officer material.

Andrew, who is well-known for his love of flying, is determined to become a naval air pilot rather than aiming for a traditional position on the bridge. Although Prince Philip and Prince Charles are both qualified pilots, Andrew will be the first in the family to specialize as an airman. The young prince has proved he is extremely fit and has all the apparent qualities required by this most demanding of service activities. Subject to passing his aptitude tests and making a formal application, the Prince will probably join the Royal Navy towards the end of 1979.

He will have seven months general naval and air training at Dartmouth, followed by ten months elementary flying tuition. He will become qualified to fly helicopters after two years, and fixed-wing jets after two and a half. It is understood that Andrew plans to apply for a twelve-year short-service commission. Although the Royal Navy will have to decide what sort of flying he shows an aptitude for, there is a large variety of aircraft available. When qualified, Andrew could find himself piloting Harrier vertical take-off fighters, helicopters, or Phantom jets.

It's just as well that Andrew is eager to enter the services, for although in theory the Prince should be free to choose any career he wishes, in practice there are problems for the young members of the royal family, as one member of the royal household explained:

'Of course, business would present some complications because royals simply do not get involved with anything having to do with advertising. So any kind of commercial thing might be difficult. A career in the army presents problems because they could never be sent to any hot spots such as Northern Ireland. Politics, too, are out, of course.'

A mature looking Prince Andrew talks to officials at a rowing club in Vancouver. He showed a keen interest in the rowing activities of the club.

In fact, one thing the Prince will not do, despite his eighteen years, will be vote. By custom none of the Queen's immediate family vote even if they have the right to do so. Prince Charles and Prince Philip are both automatically disenfranchised because they are members of the House of Lords.

It is usual for the younger sons of monarchs to be created dukes, and in all proability the Queen will follow this tradition. She may decide to bestow on Andrew the title of Duke of York, the traditional title for the sovereign's second son, and one that her father held before becoming king.

As Andrew gets older he is making more and more public appearances to help him gain experience in his role as a king's understudy. Every adult member of the royal family attends a certain number of official functions, and no doubt Andrew will eventually attend his fair share of charity film premieres, ship launchings, statue unveilings, and civic dinners.

There are still some duties that the Prince cannot undertake until he is older. For example, under the rules governing access to state papers, the secrets of the red dispatch boxes usually are read only by the Queen and Prince Charles. When the Queen is abroad, the papers are dealt with by the Counsellors of State. Prince Philip, the Queen

Mother, Princess Anne and the Duke of Gloucester are the present Counsellors, but when Prince Andrew reaches the age of 21, he will take the place of the Duke of Gloucester.

The Queen chose an international and extraordinarily public event for Prince Andrew's 'coming out' – the 1976 Olympic Games in Montreal. Until that time very little had been seen of Andrew, and the general public was immensely impressed with the young man who took such a keen interest in everything that was going on around him. Andrew wanted to see every sport he could, and even when his parents returned exhausted to their quarters, he often begged to be allowed to return to watch whatever competition was still in progress.

In 1977, while he was attending Lakefield College, Andrew took time off from his studies to join Prince Charles, who was in Calgary for the last two days of his royal tour of Canada. Calgary

Opposite and overleaf: Prince Andrew in the reviewing stand at the Calgary Stampede Parade was later joined by Prince Charles.

is the setting for an annual world-famous rodeo, and cowboys come from all over Canada and the United States to take part in it. Andrew took a front seat in the reviewing stand while his brother passed him at the head of the almost unending columns of beauty queens, cattle, cowboys and Indians that make up the magnificent Calgary Stampede Parade. When the two brothers caught each other's eyes, the smiles that spread over their faces sent the crowds screeching with delight. Later, Charles joined Andrew in the reviewing stand, each of them looking every inch a 'westerner' in their casual suits, patterned shirts, string ties and brilliant white Stetson hats.

After the parade, the two brothers went to watch the rodeo. Champion cowboys explained the various contests to them and a clutch of beautiful young women surrounded Andrew as he stood watching the riding. The girls had him penned into a corner, and he seemed to love it!

Prince Andrew and Prince Edward received a particularly enthusiastic welcome at the opening of the 1978 Commonwealth Games in Edmonton, Alberta. They drove around the arena in an open car behind their parents and waved to the packed stadium. This was the highlight of the Canadian tour in which the two princes accompanied the Queen and Prince Philip on a visit to three provinces (Newfoundland, Saskatchewan and Alberta), for the occasion enabled not only Canadians, but the entire Commonwealth to share in the royal visit.

Andrew obviously has a great affection for Canada and returned there to attend the 1978 Commonwealth Games at Edmonton with his parents and younger brother, Prince Edward. As usual, he proved an extremely popular figure and took an enthusiastic interest in all the sporting activities. After the Games, Andrew travelled to British Columbia with his father, Prince Philip, who may have been somewhat surprised and amused at the way that his young son unintentionally stole the limelight wherever he went.

Andrew has been to Europe on several occasions, but those have been mostly private visits

Andrew takes the lead when he and Charles arrive at Bromont.

during his school holidays. He has spent time in Germany and Austria to improve his command of the German language, just as he took part in an exchange visit to a French school to improve his French. In 1969 he accompanied his parents on a cruise to Norway, and is said to enjoy life on board the Royal Yacht *Britannia* very much.

He was also on *Britannia* when the Queen and Prince Philip made their visit to Northern Ireland in 1977. Andrew was allowed to join his parents when they went ashore to visit Coleraine – an unexpected treat indeed for the many local people who lined the streets.

Andrew in a pensive mood as he watches one of many events at the Commonwealth Games.

Andrew was delighted to be able to attend the Commonwealth Games at Edmonton and demonstrated his interest by visiting the competitors' village and having lunch in the cafeteria with the athletes.

Prince Andrew never seemed to tire of watching the events at the Commonwealth Games. Here he seems to share the tension of the competitors as he watches the shooting competition.

Prince Andrew, with the skyscrapers of Vancouver in the background, looks very relaxed as he waves to the cheering crowds during a private visit to British Columbia with his father, the Duke of Edinburgh.

Nevertheless he seemed quite at home and went around asking and answering questions as though he had been doing it all his life.

Later, at Lakefield, civic leader Stephen Weir told how, during a press conference, one sharp-witted photographer from a particular newspaper tried to persuade the Prince to pose for a picture wearing a ski-cap that bore the name of the newspaper.

'But the Prince realized at once he was being set up to advertise the [newspaper], so he simply folded up the cap and held it behind his back.'

Having been granted permission to come ashore in Northern Ireland, Prince Andrew made the trip from the Royal Yacht Britannia in the Queen's helicopter.

Prince Andrew is acutely aware that Britain is becoming more and more a part of Europe. He attended a seminar at Gordonstoun organized by the European Atlantic Movement and was particularly interested in the role played by individual Ministers and governments in the decision-making processes of the European Economic Community. He was described at the seminar as 'the royal family's most interested European'.

Prince Andrew may be referred to as 'the joker in the royal pack', but there is also a serious side to his nature. He has never been allowed to forget the fact that he is royal and that he is second in line to the throne. Observers speak of a well-groomed young man, quick of tongue and eye, whose mature diplomacy is more usually found in a man ten years his senior. It did not seem to take him very long to learn how to behave with the press. When he held his first press conference on his arrival in Canada to begin his studies at Lakefield College he told the waiting reporters,

'This is the first time I have done this sort of thing. I am only a nipper – I'm not considered old enough for interviews with the press.'

An official briefs Andrew in Northern Ireland.

Prince Andrew always enjoys visiting Canada and the Canadians adore him, for he always seems to find time to stop and chat.

The three jet-setting princes share a joke at the Farnborough Air Show in Kent. They dropped in to inspect aircraft and exhibitions, and to watch a flying display.

Inevitably, comparisons are drawn between Prince Charles and Prince Andrew. There obviously are many similarities in their appearances and personalities, and probably just as many differences. It may seem unfair to some extent to try to compare them at all because of the difference in their ages. Prince Andrew still has a long way to go before he can hope to achieve the remarkable urbanity and poise of his older brother, but his education and his preparation in protocol and statecraft is proving just as thorough.

Gordonstoun has succeeded in channelling Andrew's high spirits and sense of adventure into useful endeavours, and the navy will probably succeed equally well. Whatever Prince Andrew's future may hold for him, he seems to be a strong-willed young man who will want to achieve something in life that does not depend on the fact that he was born with a royal spoon in his mouth.

Andrew is following firmly in his brother's footsteps. Together they attend a parachute course and share a joke while waiting for the weather to improve.

During the Queen's three-day Jubilee tour of the West Country Prince Andrew and Prince Edward visit a tableau showing the different activities of the Royal Marines.

Overleaf: During his first official tour Prince Andrew accompanies the Queen, and walks among the crowd chatting to delighted Canadians. The tour proved a resounding success and everyone clamoured to capture the attention of the handsome young Prince.